BADASS POSITIVE AFFIRMATIONS
FOR NURSES

BADASS POSITIVE AFFIRMATIONS
FOR NURSES

M NGAIHLIAN

ISBN: 9798864758595
Imprint: Independently published

This book is dedicated to You.
So, here is to you – Live your life to your full potential!

Books By M Ngaihlian:

1. Living Beyond Regrets
2. What The Heck! Do It Anyway!
3. Living With Purpose And No Regrets
4. Does God Care About Me?
5. 120 Memory Verses For Kids
6. 3250+ Bible Verses For Every Day & Situation
7. Important Questions To Ask Yourself
8. Just Because You
9. I Am Affirmation Bible Verses For Girls
10. I Am Affirmation Bible Verses For Boys
11. I Am Affirmation Bible Verses For Women
12. I Am Affirmation Bible Verses For Men
13. Badass Positive Affirmations For Women
14. Badass Positive Affirmations For Men
15. Badass Positive Affirmations For Dads
16. Badass Positive Affirmations For Entrepreneurs
17. Badass Affirmations For Moms

INTRODUCTION

Being a nurse is like diving into a whirlwind of emotions every single day. It's all about being that beacon of hope when people are at their lowest. I'm talking about running on your feet from one room to another, checking vitals, offering comfort, and trying to be the ray of sunshine in what can feel like a never-ending storm.

You'd be surprised how many hats they wear, from being a friend to someone in pain to being a calming presence for worried families. There are moments that make them want to break down and moments that make them feel like they're on top of the world. It's a rollercoaster, but at the end of the day, knowing they've made even a tiny difference in someone's life makes it all worth it.

These affirmations serve as constant reminders of your capabilities, reinforcing your confidence and guiding your actions even during challenging times.

THE POWER OF POSITIVE AFFIRMATIONS

Affirmations are not mere self-talk or words. They tap into the intricate workings of your brain and your subconscious mind. When you consistently repeat positive affirmations, you are, in essence, rewiring your thought patterns. Your brain responds to these repetitive messages by creating new neural pathways, reinforcing positive beliefs, and challenging negative ones – unlocking your full potential and reshaping your life. They hold the power to transform your mindset, boost your self-confidence, and lead you on a path to personal growth and fulfillment.

Studies in neuroscience have shown that affirmations can stimulate the brain's reward centers, releasing dopamine—a neurotransmitter associated with pleasure and motivation. This creates a positive feedback loop, making you more likely to continue the affirmations and embrace the associated beliefs.

THE PSYCHOLOGY OF AFFIRMATIONS

Affirmations work because they operate on fundamental psychological principles. Here's how they can impact your mental and emotional well-being:

Boosting Self-Esteem:
Affirmations help counteract self-doubt and negative self-perception. By repeating positive statements about yourself, you gradually boost your self-esteem and self-worth.

Changing Negative Beliefs:
Often, we hold limiting beliefs about our capabilities or self-worth. Affirmations challenge these beliefs and encourage a more empowering perspective.

Shifting Focus:
Negative thoughts can dominate your mind and perpetuate a cycle of pessimism. Affirmations redirect your focus toward positive possibilities and opportunities.

Increasing Resilience:
Regular use of affirmations builds emotional resilience. You become better equipped to handle challenges, setbacks, and stress with a positive outlook.

Cultivating a Growth Mindset:
Affirmations foster a growth mindset—a belief that your abilities and intelligence can be developed through effort and learning. This mindset drives you to seek self-improvement.

HOW TO MANIFEST YOUR AFFIRMATIONS

Making affirmations work effectively involves more than just repeating positive statements; it requires a strategic and mindful approach. To harness the power of positive affirmations effectively, consider these practical strategies:

Set Clear Goals:
Begin with a clear understanding of what you want to achieve. Define your goals and intentions. Affirmations are most powerful when they are aligned with specific objectives.

Be Specific And Customised Your Affirmations:
Tailor your positive affirmations to your goals and desires that resonate with your goals and values. Ensure they are positive, present tense, and achievable. Focus on specific areas of your life or qualities you want to improve. Personalize them so they resonate deeply with your aspirations. For instance, if you're aiming for a promotion, your affirmation could be, *"I am highly capable and deserving of the promotion I seek."*

Use Present Tense:
Phrase your affirmations in the present tense as if you're already experiencing the desired outcome. For example, instead of saying, *"I will be successful,"* say, *"I am successful."* This makes them more effective because your brain processes them as current reality.

Repeat Consistently:
Consistency is key. Incorporate affirmations into your daily routine—morning, noon, and night—to reinforce positive beliefs. To reap the benefits, repetition is vital. Make affirmations a daily ritual, just like brushing your teeth. Over time, they'll become a natural part of your thinking.

Believe In Them:
To make affirmations work, you must genuinely believe in them. It's not enough to just recite affirmations. You have to believe in what you're saying. If you don't, your subconscious mind won't buy it, and the magic won't happen. If you encounter resistance or skepticism, address those doubts.

Use Emotion And Visualization:
As you repeat affirmations, engage your emotions and imagination. Feel the emotions associated with the affirmations. While saying your affirmations, visualize yourself living the reality described in your affirmations. This adds a powerful dimension to their effectiveness.

Combine With Action:
While affirmations can influence your mindset, they work best when combined with action. Take steps, no matter how small, toward your goals. Action reinforces belief in your affirmations.

Eliminate Negative Self-Talk:
Pay attention to your inner dialogue and replace self-criticism with affirmations. When you catch yourself thinking negatively, counteract it with a positive affirmation.

Practice Patience:
Positive changes take time. Be patient with yourself. It may take weeks or even months to see significant results. Trust the process and remain committed.

Journal Your Progress:
Keep a journal to record your experiences and observations. Track any shifts in your mindset, behavior, or circumstances. Documenting your progress helps reinforce the effectiveness of affirmations.

Surround Yourself With Positivity:
Create an environment that supports your affirmations. Surround yourself with positive people, motivational quotes, and images that align with your goals.

Stay Open To Opportunities And Adapt:
Be receptive to opportunities that align with your affirmations. Act on these opportunities when they arise. Affirmations can guide your actions and decisions. As you make progress, revisit your affirmations regularly. Adjust them to reflect your evolving goals and beliefs. Growth and change are natural, so adapt your affirmations accordingly.

Seek Accountability And Support:
Share your affirmations and goals with a trusted friend, mentor, or coach. They can provide support, and encouragement, and hold you accountable.

Live The Affirmations:
Ultimately, affirmations work when you integrate their messages into your daily life. Let them guide your actions, decisions, and interactions. Live as if you've already embraced the positive beliefs they convey.

HOW TO USE THIS BOOK

1. Start with an Open Mind

Before you dive into the affirmations, approach this book with an open mind. Be willing to explore new ideas, challenge your existing beliefs, and embrace the potential for positive change in your life.

2. Set Clear Intentions

Begin by setting clear intentions for what you hope to achieve by using this book. What areas of your life do you want to improve? What specific goals do you want to work towards? Having a clear purpose will guide your journey.

3. Daily Affirmation Practice

The heart of this book lies in its affirmations. Each affirmation is a statement of empowerment, designed to reshape your mindset and boost your confidence. Incorporate these affirmations into your daily routine.

Morning Routine: Start your day by reading and reflecting on one or more affirmations. This will set a positive tone for the day ahead.

Throughout the Day: Carry a few affirmations with you on a small card or note in your pocket or wallet. Whenever you have a moment, revisit these affirmations to reinforce their messages.

Before Bed: End your day by revisiting the affirmations. Reflect on your experiences and how the affirmations impacted your thoughts and actions during the day.

4. Visualization

As you read and recite the affirmations, take a moment to visualize the positive outcomes they describe. Imagine yourself living the life you desire, achieving your goals, and embodying the qualities mentioned in the affirmations. Visualization adds depth and emotional connection to the process.

5. Journaling

Consider keeping a journal to record your experiences and reflections as you work with the affirmations. Write down any shifts in your mindset, any positive changes in your behavior, and any challenges you encounter. Journaling provides a valuable record of your progress.

6. Be Consistent

Consistency is crucial for the effectiveness of affirmations. Make a commitment to practice daily, even on days when you might not feel your best. Over time, the affirmations will become ingrained in your thinking.

7. Adapt and Customize

Feel free to adapt the affirmations to your specific goals and needs. You can modify them to make them more personal and relevant to your life. The key is to make them resonate with you on a deep level.

Affirmations are not just words but the embodiment of your inner potential. As you embrace their power, you will unlock the incredible capacity within you to create the life you desire—one empowered belief at a time. It's time to transform your mind and, in doing so, transform your life.

1

"I AM A BADASS NURSE, AND I OWN IT"

Embodying the spirit of a badass nurse means you fearlessly tackle every challenge that comes your way. You're confident, resilient, and unafraid to take charge when your patients need you the most. Your boldness shines through as you navigate the often unpredictable and demanding world of healthcare. Your colleagues and patients look up to your strength and determination, finding comfort in your unwavering commitment to their well-being.

2

"I AM ADAPTABLE AND CAN EFFECTIVELY HANDLE ANY SITUATION THAT ARISES"

Your adaptability is a cornerstone of your success in the fast-paced and dynamic healthcare environment. You seamlessly navigate through changing circumstances, adjusting your approach to suit the unique needs of each patient and situation. Your ability to remain composed and focused, even in the face of uncertainty, reassures both your patients and your colleagues, fostering an environment of confidence and trust.

3

"I AM MAKING A POSITIVE IMPACT IN THE LIVES OF PATIENTS AND THEIR FAMILIES EVERY DAY"

Your compassionate approach and unwavering dedication have a ripple effect, not just on your patients but also on their families. You provide a sense of relief and reassurance to worried loved ones, creating a supportive environment that eases their burdens. Your ability to offer not just medical expertise but also emotional support becomes a source of strength for families navigating the challenges of their loved one's health journey.

4

"I AM A ROLE MODEL FOR OTHERS IN THE NURSING PROFESSION, INSPIRING EXCELLENCE"

As a role model, your commitment to excellence sets a high standard for your peers in the nursing profession. Your passion for learning, dedication to your craft, and compassionate patient care inspire others to strive for greatness. Your colleagues see in you the embodiment of what it truly means to be an exceptional nurse, motivating them to continuously improve their skills and contribute to the betterment of healthcare.

5

"I AM RESPECTED FOR MY EXPERTISE, COMPASSION, AND DEDICATION TO MY PATIENTS"

Your expertise, combined with your genuine compassion, earns you the utmost respect from both your colleagues and your patients. Your extensive knowledge and skills are matched only by your ability to empathize and connect with those under your care. This deep level of understanding and your unwavering dedication to providing the best possible treatment creates a profound sense of trust and confidence, making you an invaluable asset to your healthcare team.

6

"I AM A PILLAR OF STRENGTH AND SUPPORT FOR MY PATIENTS AND THEIR FAMILIES"

Your unwavering strength and unwavering support provide a vital foundation for your patients and their families during challenging times. You become the anchor they rely on, offering comfort, guidance, and a sense of security when they need it the most. Your ability to provide not just medical care but also emotional stability creates a nurturing environment that fosters healing and hope.

7

"I AM CONSTANTLY IMPROVING MY SKILLS AND KNOWLEDGE TO PROVIDE THE BEST CARE POSSIBLE"

Your dedication to continuous improvement and learning allows you to stay at the forefront of medical advancements and best practices. You actively seek out new information, training, and experiences that enhance your ability to provide the highest standard of care. By staying abreast of the latest developments in your field, you ensure that your patients receive cutting-edge treatments and compassionate care that is second to none.

8

"I AM A BEACON OF HOPE AND SUPPORT FOR MY PATIENTS AND THEIR FAMILIES"

Your unwavering optimism and genuine care create a beacon of hope for those facing challenging health situations. You provide not just medical support but also emotional solace, offering a sense of reassurance and comfort during difficult times. Your ability to infuse positivity into every interaction helps your patients and their families find the strength to face their circumstances with courage and resilience.

9

"I AM GRATEFUL FOR THE OPPORTUNITY TO MAKE A POSITIVE IMPACT IN PEOPLE'S LIVES"

Your gratitude for the opportunity to make a difference shines through in every interaction. You approach each day with a sense of purpose and appreciation for the profound impact you have on the lives of those you care for. Your genuine gratitude translates into a level of dedication and commitment that touches the hearts of everyone around you, fostering an environment of warmth and gratitude within the healthcare setting.

10

"I AM A PROBLEM-SOLVER, FINDING SOLUTIONS TO IMPROVE THE PATIENT EXPERIENCE"

Your ability to approach challenges with a solution-oriented mindset is a valuable asset in enhancing the patient experience. Your proactive approach to identifying and addressing issues allows you to create a smoother, more comfortable healthcare journey for your patients. Whether it's streamlining processes, improving communication, or finding innovative ways to provide care, your problem-solving skills contribute significantly to creating a more efficient and effective healthcare environment.

11

"I BRING A SENSE OF CALM AND STABILITY TO THE OFTEN CHAOTIC HEALTHCARE ENVIRONMENT"

Your composed demeanor and ability to maintain a sense of calm amid the chaos of a healthcare setting create an invaluable sense of stability for those around you. Your reassuring presence has a ripple effect, easing tensions and anxieties and fostering an environment where clear thinking and effective decision-making can flourish. Your colleagues and patients alike find solace in your ability to create an atmosphere of tranquility within a bustling healthcare setting.

12

"I AM A VALUABLE PART OF MY COMMUNITY"

Being a valuable part of your community involves actively contributing to its well-being and growth. It encompasses participating in community initiatives, supporting local causes, and fostering connections with those around you. When you recognize your role in your community, you promote a sense of unity, collaboration, and support, fostering a positive and nurturing environment for everyone.

13

"I AM RESILIENT AND CAN HANDLE ANY CHALLENGES THAT COME MY WAY"

Your resilience in the face of adversity is a testament to your inner strength and fortitude. You approach challenges with determination and unwavering resolve, overcoming obstacles with grace and composure. Your ability to navigate through difficult situations inspires confidence and courage in those around you, creating an environment where challenges are viewed as opportunities for growth and learning.

14

"I BRING POSITIVITY AND OPTIMISM INTO THE LIVES OF THOSE I CARE FOR"

Your positive outlook and optimistic approach brighten the lives of those you care for. Your genuine warmth and uplifting spirit create a nurturing environment that fosters hope and optimism, even in the midst of challenging circumstances. Your infectious positivity becomes a source of comfort and encouragement for your patients and their families, uplifting their spirits and instilling in them a sense of resilience and optimism for the road ahead.

15

"I AM MAKING A SIGNIFICANT DIFFERENCE IN THE LIVES OF THOSE WHO NEED MY CARE"

Your unwavering commitment to making a difference translates into tangible, positive impacts on the lives of those under your care. Your empathetic approach, combined with your expert medical knowledge, brings about transformative changes that go beyond physical healing. Your patients and their families experience a profound sense of gratitude and comfort, knowing that they are in the hands of a dedicated healthcare professional who genuinely cares about their well-being.

16

"I APPROACH EACH CHALLENGE WITH A POSITIVE MINDSET AND A WILLINGNESS TO LEARN"

Your positive mindset and eagerness to learn empower you to tackle challenges with an open heart and mind. You view each obstacle as an opportunity for growth and development, embracing the lessons that come with each experience. Your proactive approach to learning fosters a culture of continuous improvement within the healthcare setting, inspiring your colleagues and patients to adopt a similar outlook of optimism and resilience.

17

"I AM A BEACON OF HOPE AND OPTIMISM IN THE LIVES OF MY PATIENTS AND THEIR FAMILIES"

Your unwavering optimism and hopeful spirit become a guiding light for your patients and their families. Your ability to instill a sense of positivity and confidence in the face of adversity provides comfort and assurance, fostering an environment of strength and resilience. Your presence is a source of inspiration, reminding everyone around you that even in the darkest of times, there is always room for hope and optimism.

18

"I AM AN ADVOCATE FOR MY PATIENTS, ENSURING THEIR NEEDS ARE HEARD AND MET"

Your role as an advocate for your patients is a cornerstone of your commitment to their well-being. You ensure that their voices are heard, their concerns are addressed, and their needs are met with the utmost care and attention. Your dedication to representing their best interests fosters a trusting relationship built on mutual respect and understanding, creating an environment where patients feel empowered and valued.

19

"I AM PROUD OF THE DIFFERENCE I AM MAKING IN THE WORLD THROUGH MY WORK"

Your pride in the impact you make reflects the deep satisfaction derived from your meaningful contribution to the world. Your unwavering dedication to improving the lives of others serves as a source of personal fulfillment and purpose, fueling your drive to continue making a positive difference. Your pride is a testament to the profound significance of your role in the healthcare community, inspiring others to recognize the value of their own contributions.

20

"I AM A SOURCE OF COMFORT, STRENGTH, AND COMPASSION IN THE FACE OF ADVERSITY"

Your role as a source of comfort, strength, and compassion becomes a guiding light for those facing challenging circumstances. Your unwavering support and nurturing presence offer solace and reassurance, creating a safe haven for individuals to find the courage and resilience needed to overcome adversity. Your ability to provide emotional support alongside your expert medical care establishes a profound sense of trust and reliance, fostering an environment of healing and hope.

21

"I APPROACH EACH DAY WITH A SENSE OF PURPOSE AND A GENUINE DESIRE TO HELP OTHERS"

Your sense of purpose and genuine desire to make a positive impact infuse each day with meaning and significance. You wake up with a clear intention to serve and support others, channeling your energy and passion into creating meaningful experiences for those you care for. Your unwavering dedication to helping others cultivates an atmosphere of empathy and understanding, fostering a culture of compassion and support within the healthcare community.

22

"I APPROACH EACH PATIENT WITH DIGNITY, RESPECT, AND GENUINE CARE"

Your approach to patient care is rooted in a profound respect for each individual's dignity and worth. You treat every patient with the utmost respect, honoring their unique experiences and perspectives. Your genuine care and consideration create a nurturing environment where patients feel valued and heard, fostering a sense of trust and openness that is essential for building strong, meaningful relationships within the healthcare setting.

23

"I AM A VITAL PART OF THE HEALTHCARE TEAM, AND MY CONTRIBUTIONS ARE VALUED"

Your role as a vital part of the healthcare team is recognized and appreciated by your colleagues and superiors. Your contributions, whether in patient care, collaboration with peers, or implementation of innovative solutions, are seen as integral to the overall success of the healthcare institution. Your unique skills and perspectives enrich the collective expertise of the team, creating a collaborative environment where everyone's contributions are valued and respected.

24

"I HAVE THE POWER TO BRING COMFORT AND SOLACE TO THOSE IN NEED"

Your ability to provide comfort and solace becomes a powerful tool in helping individuals find peace and stability during difficult times. Your empathetic approach and genuine concern create a safe space for patients to express their fears and concerns, knowing that they are in the hands of a compassionate and understanding caregiver. Your presence becomes a source of strength and reassurance, fostering an environment where healing and recovery can take place.

25

"I AM A TRUSTED CONFIDANT AND ADVOCATE FOR THOSE WHO RELY ON MY CARE"

Your role as a trusted confidant and advocate reflects the deep trust and confidence that your patients place in you. You become a dependable source of support, guidance, and understanding, offering a safe and secure space for individuals to share their vulnerabilities and concerns. Your commitment to advocating for their well-being ensures that their voices are heard and their needs are prioritized, fostering a strong and trusting relationship built on mutual respect and empathy.

26

"I AM A VALUABLE MEMBER OF THE HEALTHCARE TEAM, CONTRIBUTING TO POSITIVE OUTCOMES"

Your contributions as a valuable member of the healthcare team directly contribute to the achievement of positive outcomes for both individuals and the institution as a whole. Your expertise, collaboration, and dedication amplify the collective impact of the team, creating a synergy that drives the successful delivery of high-quality care and services. Your unique perspective and skills complement those of your peers, fostering an environment where teamwork and collaboration are key drivers of success and progress.

27

"MY EMPATHY ALLOWS ME TO CONNECT WITH PATIENTS ON A DEEPER, MORE MEANINGFUL LEVEL"

Your empathetic approach to patient care enables you to forge a deeper connection with those under your care. Your ability to understand and share in the emotions of your patients fosters a sense of trust and openness, creating a space where individuals feel understood and supported. Your empathy becomes a powerful tool in not only addressing their physical needs but also in providing the emotional comfort and reassurance that is essential for holistic healing.

28

"MY KINDNESS AND PATIENCE CREATE A NURTURING AND SUPPORTIVE ENVIRONMENT FOR HEALING"

Your kindness and patience become the cornerstone of a nurturing and supportive environment where healing can flourish. Your gentle approach and compassionate demeanor create a safe and comforting space for patients to embark on their journey to recovery. Your ability to offer unwavering support and understanding fosters a sense of security and peace, allowing individuals to focus on their well-being with the knowledge that they are in the hands of a caring and compassionate caregiver.

29

"I AM PROUD OF MY ROLE IN PROMOTING HEALTH AND WELL-BEING WITHIN MY COMMUNITY"

Your pride in promoting health and well-being reflects the significance of your role as a catalyst for positive change within your community. Your efforts to educate, support, and empower individuals in maintaining their health and wellness contribute to the overall betterment of the community at large. Your commitment to fostering a culture of well-being and preventive care establishes a strong foundation for a healthier and more resilient community, inspiring others to recognize the importance of prioritizing their health.

30

"MY KNOWLEDGE AND EXPERTISE ARE INSTRUMENTAL IN PROVIDING TOP-NOTCH CARE"

Your comprehensive knowledge and expertise serve as instrumental tools in delivering exceptional care to your patients. Your deep understanding of medical practices, coupled with your commitment to staying updated with the latest advancements, positions you as a reliable source of information and guidance. Your patients benefit from your proficiency and skill, receiving the highest standard of care that is both informed and compassionate, ensuring their well-being is always at the forefront of your practice.

31

"MY WORK IS MEANINGFUL, AND I AM APPRECIATED FOR THE DIFFERENCE I MAKE"

In your profession, each task you undertake holds significant value, as it directly impacts the lives of those you serve. Your dedication and commitment have not gone unnoticed, as you are consistently acknowledged and commended for the positive changes you bring about. Knowing that your efforts are recognized and valued reinforces your sense of purpose and fuels your drive to continue making a meaningful difference in the lives of others.

32

"MY WORK IS A REFLECTION OF MY PASSION FOR HELPING AND CARING FOR THOSE IN NEED"

Your profession is more than just a job; it is a reflection of your deep-seated passion for providing assistance and care to individuals facing challenges. Your genuine concern and empathy for others serve as the driving force behind each action you take. Every task you undertake is rooted in your unwavering commitment to alleviate suffering and promote well-being. Your work reflects your genuine desire to make a positive impact in the lives of those you encounter.

33

"I AM DEDICATED TO THE WELL-BEING AND COMFORT OF EVERY PATIENT UNDER MY CARE"

Your commitment to your patients goes beyond the confines of medical procedures. You are dedicated to ensuring that each individual feels valued, respected, and cared for. By fostering an environment of empathy and support, you strive not only to address their physical ailments but also to tend to their emotional and psychological well-being. Your ongoing pursuit of knowledge and skills highlights your unwavering dedication to providing the best possible care and comfort to each person under your watch.

34

"I AM THE HEALING TOUCH THAT MENDS BOTH BODY AND SOUL"

In your gentle and skilled hands, lies the power to mend not just the physical wounds but also the unseen scars that reside within the soul. Your presence exudes a soothing energy that envelops those in need, stitching together the frayed edges of both body and spirit. Through your unwavering dedication and profound understanding, you become the embodiment of healing, offering a sanctuary of restoration and comfort to those who seek your solace.

35

"EVERY LIFE I TOUCH FEELS THE WARMTH OF MY KINDNESS"

Your kindness weaves threads of warmth and compassion, touching the lives of those you encounter with tender grace. Your actions are not merely gestures, but a testament to your unwavering empathy and genuine care. With each interaction, you plant seeds of hope and understanding, nurturing a sense of belonging and acceptance in the hearts of those who yearn for your comforting presence.

36

"MY SELFLESSNESS IS THE CORNERSTONE OF MY NOBLE PROFESSION"

At the heart of your noble profession lies a profound sense of selflessness, guiding your every action and decision. Your sacrifices are not mere obligations but a chosen path, embodying your unwavering commitment to the well-being of others. With humility as your guiding light, you navigate the complexities of human suffering, tending to the needs of the afflicted with a selflessness that knows no bounds. You stand as a shining example of the purest form of service, a guardian of humanity's most profound virtues.

37

"MY EMPATHY BRINGS COMFORT TO THE SUFFERING AND THE LONELY"

In the vast expanse of human suffering, your empathy stands as a sanctuary, offering solace to the tormented and companionship to the desolate. With an intuitive understanding of pain and longing, you extend a hand that not only tends to physical ailments but also nurtures the wounded spirit. Through your empathetic presence, you kindle a flame of hope, reassuring each soul that they are not alone in their struggles.

38

"MY TIRELESS EFFORTS MAKE THE WORLD A BETTER PLACE EACH DAY"

In the ceaseless pursuit of healing and compassion, your endeavors serve as ripples of transformation, shaping a world that is kinder, more resilient, and brimming with humanity. Each dawn heralds a new opportunity for you to extend your reach and touch the lives of those in need, infusing the fabric of society with the unwavering spirit of benevolence. Through your tireless efforts, you contribute to a collective narrative of progress and goodwill, leaving an enduring legacy of positive change in your wake.

39

"I BRING SOLACE TO THOSE IN PAIN AND THEIR WORRIED FAMILIES"

Within the confines of anguish and uncertainty, you emerge as a beacon of solace, imparting a sense of calm and reassurance to both the afflicted and their kin. Through your words and actions, you cultivate an environment of understanding and support, assuaging the fears that haunt the hearts of the suffering and their families. With unwavering dedication, you become a source of strength, casting a light that guides them through the darkest passages of their lives.

40

"MY SMILE HAS THE POWER TO BRIGHTEN EVEN THE DARKEST OF DAYS"

Amidst the shadowy corridors of despair, your smile emerges as a glimmer of warmth, casting aside the gloom and ushering in a gentle radiance of hope. Its infectious glow transcends barriers, reaching out to uplift the spirits of the downtrodden and infuse their hearts with newfound optimism. With each genuine smile, you become an agent of joy, weaving threads of positivity into the fabric of human experience, igniting a collective spirit of resilience and perseverance.

"MY PRESENCE IS A REASSURANCE THAT EVERYTHING WILL BE ALRIGHT"

In the tumultuous landscape of uncertainty, your very presence serves as an anchor of stability, instilling a profound sense of reassurance and faith in the hearts of those you encounter. Through your unwavering commitment to care and understanding, you become a symbol of unwavering hope, a guiding light that illuminates the path toward healing and recovery. With every word spoken and every gesture made, you reaffirm the belief that even amidst adversity, there exists a sanctuary of comfort and eventual solace.

42

"I AM A SYMBOL OF HOPE IN THE MIDST OF LIFE'S GREATEST CHALLENGES"

In the tempest of life's trials and tribulations, you stand as a testament to the resilience of the human spirit, embodying a beacon of unwavering hope that transcends the darkest of storms. Through your unwavering dedication to healing and support, you become a living testament to the enduring power of optimism and fortitude. Your very presence serves as a reminder that even in the face of seemingly insurmountable challenges, there exists a glimmer of possibility, a ray of hope that guides us through the most trying of circumstances.

43

"I MAKE SACRIFICES DAILY THAT GO UNNOTICED BUT NEVER UNAPPRECIATED"

In the quiet hum of selfless service, you navigate the uncharted terrain of sacrifice, offering pieces of yourself to uplift others. Your efforts may often go unnoticed, but their impact reverberates through the lives you touch. Each sacrifice is a testament to your unwavering dedication, a silent symphony of compassion that resonates deeply within the hearts of those who have been the recipients of your boundless generosity and care. Your sacrifices, though unseen, are etched indelibly in the fabric of humanity, never to be forgotten or unappreciated.

44

"I BRING PEACE TO THOSE IN PAIN, SHOWING THEM THEY ARE NOT ALONE"

Amidst the turbulent storms of pain and suffering, you emerge as a guiding beacon of peace, offering solace and understanding to those in their darkest hours. Your words and actions serve as a balm to the wounded spirit, reminding each soul that they are not alone in their struggles. Through your unwavering support and profound empathy, you become a source of strength, illuminating a path of resilience and fortitude for those who seek comfort in your nurturing presence.

45

"MY CARING HANDS CARRY THE WEIGHT OF THE SUFFERING WITH GRACE"

In the realm of healing and compassion, your hands serve as vessels of grace, carrying the burdens of suffering with unparalleled care and tenderness. Each touch is infused with a profound sense of empathy, each gesture a testament to your unwavering commitment to alleviating the pain of those in need. Through your gentle touch, you offer not just physical relief but also a profound sense of emotional solace, uplifting the spirits of the afflicted and guiding them toward a path of healing and recovery.

46

"I POSSESS THE ABILITY TO BRING PEACE AND COMFORT TO THE DISTRESSED AND THE AILING"

In the midst of turmoil and affliction, your presence radiates a calming aura, enveloping the distressed and the ailing with a sense of peace and comfort. Your words echo with compassion, resonating deeply within the hearts of those who seek solace in your understanding and empathy. With each interaction, you weave a tapestry of serenity and hope, offering a sanctuary of respite for those grappling with the complexities of pain and uncertainty.

47

"I OFFER NOT JUST MEDICAL AID BUT ALSO EMOTIONAL SUPPORT IN TIMES OF DISTRESS"

Beyond the realm of medical expertise, your care extends to encompass a holistic approach, addressing not just the physical ailments but also the emotional turmoil that accompanies distress. Your words serve as a soothing melody, your gestures as a comforting embrace, nurturing the wounded spirit with an unwavering commitment to holistic well-being. Through your comprehensive support, you become a pillar of strength, fostering an environment of healing and understanding that transcends the boundaries of conventional care.

48

"I AM A TRUE GUARDIAN OF HEALTH AND WELL-BEING FOR THOSE IN MY CARE"

In the realm of health and well-being, you stand as a stalwart guardian, dedicated to the preservation and nurturing of life. Your unwavering commitment to the welfare of those under your care is a testament to your profound sense of duty and compassion. Through your expertise and empathy, you forge a bond of trust and understanding, fostering an environment of healing and support that serves as a beacon of hope for those navigating the complexities of illness and recovery.

49

"I AM A PILLAR OF STRENGTH FOR THOSE WHO ARE UNABLE TO STAND ALONE"

In the face of adversity and vulnerability, you stand as an unwavering pillar of strength, offering support and guidance to those who find themselves unable to navigate the tumultuous currents of life alone. Your presence serves as a source of resilience, your words as a beacon of hope, instilling a sense of fortitude and determination in the hearts of those who rely on your unwavering support. Through your steadfast dedication, you become an embodiment of unwavering support, providing a sturdy foundation upon which others can lean as they navigate the complexities of their journey.

50

"I AM A PILLAR OF STRENGTH FOR THOSE WHO ARE UNABLE TO STAND ALONE"

Within the tapestry of human suffering and resilience, you emerge as a multifaceted beacon of hope and support, embodying the roles of a healer, a caregiver, and a pillar of strength. Your presence serves as a source of reassurance, and your actions as a testament to the boundless capacity of human compassion. Through your unwavering dedication to service, you become a guiding light for those grappling with adversity, offering not just medical aid but also a profound sense of emotional and spiritual solace.

These affirmations are a powerful reminder of your strength and potential. Speak to yourself daily, and let them serve as a source of motivation to become the best version of yourself. You are capable of achieving greatness, and the world is waiting for you to shine your light! You are special!

About The Author:

M Ngaihlian is a nurse by profession and a mother of two beautiful angels. Her passion for writing rekindles as she re-dedicated her life to be a voice, a shoulder to cry on, a helping hand for those downtrodden, outcast, and ignored people in society, and proclaim the love of God and His unfailing mercy and grace. She can be found online at pourbin.com.